CONTENDING FOR THE FAITH

*Bible Study Notes on
The Epistle of Jude*

**Titles in the
Bible Study Notes Series**

*Everything We Need: Ephesians
Contending for the Faith: Jude*

CONTENDING FOR THE FAITH

*Bible Study Notes on
The Epistle of Jude*

Glen A. Blanscet

Copyright © 2020 by Glen A. Blanscet
Carrollton, Texas // www.glenblanscet.com

Cover Design by Georgia Rutherford
Author Photo by Becky Blanscet

All rights reserved. No part of this book may be used or reproduced by any means, graphic, electronic, or mechanical, including photocopying, recording, taping, or by any information storage retrieval system without the written permission of the author except in the case of brief quotations embodied in critical articles and reviews.

Because of the dynamic nature of the Internet, any web addresses or links contained in this book may have changed since publication
and may no longer be valid.

Printed in the United States of America

ISBN: 978-1-7344578-0-3 (paperback)
ISBN: 978-1-7344578-1-0 (e-book)
Library of Congress Control Number: 2020904142

Version date: July 2020

All Scripture quotations, unless otherwise indicated, are taken from the Holy Bible, New International Version®, NIV®. Copyright ©1973, 1978, 1984, 2011 by Biblica, Inc.™ Used by permission of Zondervan. All rights reserved worldwide. www.zondervan.com. The "NIV" and "New International Version" are trademarks registered in the United States Patent and Trademark Office by Biblica, Inc.™

Scripture quotations marked "CEV" are from the Contemporary English Version Copyright © 1991, 1992, 1995 by American Bible Society. Used by Permission.

Scripture quotations marked "CSB" are taken from the Christian Standard Bible®, Copyright © 2017 by Holman Bible Publishers. Used by permission. Christian Standard Bible®, and CSB® are federally registered trademarks of Holman Bible Publishers.

Scripture quotations marked "ESV" are taken from The Holy Bible, English Standard Version® (ESV®) Copyright © 2001 by Crossway, a publishing ministry of Good News Publishers. Used by permission. All rights reserved.
ESV Text Edition: 2016.

Scripture quotations marked "NASB" are taken from the NEW AMERICAN STANDARD® (NASB), Copyright © 1960, 1962, 1963, 1968, 1971, 1972, 1973, 1975, 1977, 1995 by The Lockman Foundation. Used by permission.

Scripture quotations marked "NKJV" are taken from the New King James Version. Copyright © 1982 by Thomas Nelson, Inc. Used by permission.
All rights reserved.

Scripture quotations marked "REB" are taken from the Revised English Bible, copyright © Cambridge University Press and Oxford University Press 1989.
All rights reserved.

I felt compelled to write and urge you

to contend for the faith that was once for all

entrusted to God's holy people.

-- Jude 3

Table of Contents

Introduction xi
Outline of the Epistle of Jude xiii

Chapter I   Introduction to the Epistle of Jude
                  (Jude 1-2)... 1

Chapter II   Warnings about False Teachers
                  (Jude 3-16)... 11

Chapter III Strategies for Contending for the Faith
                  (Jude 17-23) 39

Chapter IV Doxology
                  (Jude 24-25) 55

Notes 61
Sources Cited 73
Also by the Author 77

Introduction

TODAY'S HEADLINES REFLECT A WORLD in moral chaos and disarray, not only in secular society but also in the Christian church. Christians are bombarded daily with challenges to their faith, some of which come directly from those who oppose Christianity and some indirectly from the cultural influences and viewpoints that are inconsistent with and hostile to the teachings of Christian scripture.

From a believer's perspective, it may seem the world has never been further from God. But almost two thousand years ago, early Christian believers faced similar threats to their faith, grappling with contradictory teachings over Christian doctrine and struggling to live out their faith in a manner consistent with that doctrine.

Enter Jude. As an itinerant preacher and pastor, Jude travelled among several of the churches of the first century. One day, he began to write an encouraging letter to some of the churches he had visited, but his plans changed. He was startled by news that those churches were besieged by false teachers who were leading them away from the truth of God's grace and enticing them to live in a manner inconsistent with God's commands. So his letter took up a different topic and conveyed a heightened sense of urgency. He urged them to fight against these false teachings, to oppose those who were trying to deceive them, and to contend for their faith.

Bible Study Notes on Jude

Jude pulled no punches when he described the false teachers and the evil they taught. He encouraged believers in the churches to recognize the true nature of these false teachers, and he outlined a specific strategy for how to deal with the false teachers and those who were misled or being misled by them.

In our time, there is no more relevant message for Christians than the message of Jude. As believers, he called us to "contend for the faith," so it is essential we understand what we are fighting against and how to respond to those who attack the basic doctrines and teachings of the Christian faith.

* * * * *

This book provides, in an outline format, the notes I developed during my study of the book of Jude as I prepared to teach it to others. My hope is that these notes will provide you with some basic insights into this important letter, helping you better understand the message of Jude and its application for your own life.

Glen A. Blanscet
www.glenblanscet.com

Outline of
The Epistle of Jude

I. **Jude 1-2 – Introductory Issues**
   A. Authorship (v. 1a)
   B. Recipients (vv. 1b-2)

II. **Jude 3-16 – Warnings about False Teachers**
   A. Contending for the Faith (vv. 3-4)
   B. Describing the False Teachers (vv. 5-16)
      1. Their Immorality (vv. 5-10)
         a. The Example of the Israelites in the Wilderness (v. 5)
         b. The Example of Fallen Angels (v. 6)
         c. The Example of Sodom and Gomorrah (v. 7)
         d. Application to the False Teachers (vv. 8-10)
      2. Their Deception of Others (vv. 11-13)
         a. The Example of Cain (v. 11a)
         b. The Example of Balaam (v. 11b)
         c. The Example of Korah (v. 11c)
         d. Application to the False Teachers (vv. 12-13)
      3. Their Arrogance (vv. 14-16)
         a. A Quotation from 1 Enoch (vv. 14-15)
         b. Application to the False Teachers (v. 16)

III. Jude 17-23 – Strategies for Contending for the Faith
    A. Remember What God's Word Says (vv. 17-19)
    B. Strengthen Your Spiritual Walk (vv. 20-21)
        1. Build Yourself Up in the Faith (v. 20a)
        2. Pray in the Holy Spirit (v. 20b)
        3. Keep in God's Love (v. 21a)
        4. Wait Expectantly for God's Return (v. 21b)
    C. Engage Those Who Are Misled (vv. 22-23)
        1. Be Merciful to the Doubters (v. 22)
        2. Rescue the Deceived (v. 23a)
        3. Be Cautious with the Deceivers (v. 23b)

IV. Jude 24-25 – Doxology
    A. The Ability of God (v. 24)
    B. The Attributes of God (v. 25)

Chapter I

Introduction to The Epistle of Jude
Jude 1-2

A. *Background of the Letter.* Someone once referred to the Epistle of Jude as the "least known and most neglected book in the New Testament."[1]

1. It is one of the shortest books in the Bible, written by a man who is virtually unknown to readers today. Furthermore, it contains harsh and strange-sounding language that is difficult to understand with only a casual reading.

2. Yet, it is a highly significant and important Christian document that is decidedly relevant to Christian lives today. In its succinct and pointed way, this short letter highlights the distinction between Christian and secular teachings and accentuates the important connection that exists between our beliefs and our conduct.

3. Consequently, the book of Jude is an important warning against nominal Christians who are easily recognized by their hypocrisy (i.e., claiming to be a Christian without living Christian values) or their complacency (i.e., failing to stand strong for the truth of Christian doctrine against the attacks of a pagan world).[2] Instead of such an insincere and weak Christianity, Jude called us to live

our Christian lives in a strong, dynamic, and committed manner.

B. *Authorship* **(Jude 1a).** The author identified himself in the first verse of the letter as "Jude, a servant of Jesus Christ and a brother of James."

1. There are at least six different men in the New Testament who were named Jude (or Judas), but there is little dispute among commentators that the author of this

The Six Judes in the New Testament		
Judas Iscariot	Matthew 10:4, 27:1-3 Mark 3:19 Luke 6:16, 22:3-6, 47	The apostle who betrayed Jesus and hanged himself
Judas, son of James	Luke 6:16 Acts 1:13	An apostle of Jesus's, also known as Thaddaeus (Matthew 10:3; Mark 3:18)
Judas, the Galilean	Acts 5:37	A revolutionary who led a revolt against Roman taxation during Quirinius's census around 6 A.D.
Judas of Damascus	Acts 9:11	The owner of the house on Straight Street where Saul went after his road to Damascus experience with Jesus
Judas Barsabbas	Acts 15:22, 27, 32	One of the prophets sent by the Jerusalem church to accompany Paul and Barnabas to the church in Antioch
Jude, the brother of Jesus and James	Matthew 13:55 Mark 6:3	A son of Joseph and Mary and brother to Jesus, James, Joseph, and Simon

letter is the brother of Jesus and of James, the leader of the Jerusalem church.[3]

a. Rather than identify himself as the brother of Jesus, Jude called himself "a servant of Jesus Christ."

   (1) While this may have been an act of humility on Jude's part, it more likely was intended to convey his authority for what he was writing. Being the brother of Jesus did not convey any spiritual benefit to Jude. His ministry and work on behalf of Christ did.[4]

   > **What is the significance of the phrase "servant of Jesus Christ"?**

   (2) Besides simply being a title that added authority to what he wrote, Jude's reference to himself as "a servant of Jesus Christ" has important theological meaning. In the Old Testament, Moses was called "the servant of the Lord" (Joshua 14:7; 2 Kings 18:12), and David was also referred to as the Lord's servant (Psalm 18 superscription; Ezekiel 34:23). For Jude to use the same phrase but replace the Lord's name with Jesus Christ is significant because it showed that the early Christians had no problem equating Jesus with the God of the Old Testament.[5]

b. Jude also described himself as a "brother of James." This reference was probably made for identification purposes because James was a well-known figure among Christians at the time.

2. We do not know a lot about Jude from either the Bible or early Church history other than the following facts:

   a. He was one of four brothers of Jesus (Matthew 13:55, Mark 6:3).[6]

   b. Like all of Jesus' brothers, Jude did not believe Jesus was the Messiah prior to His resurrection (Mark 3:21; John 7:5; Acts 1:14).

   c. Jude may have been an itinerant missionary who traveled with his wife to spread the teachings of Christ (1 Corinthians 9:5).

   d. The only early Church reference to Jude was a mention of his grandchildren. Hegesippus, an early second-century Church historian, told a story about Jude's grandchildren being brought before Emperor Domitian who heard they were descendants of the Davidic line and thus were a potential political threat. However, upon learning they owned very little property and were merely hard-working farmers, as revealed by their calloused hands, he determined they were "of no account" and let them go.[7]

C. *Recipients* **(Jude 1b-2).** Jude identified his recipients as "those who have been called, who are loved in God the Father and kept for Jesus Christ."

   1. Clearly, the recipients of the letter were believers, but otherwise there is no evidence regarding who the readers of the letter were or whether they were primarily of Jewish or Gentile background. The most plausible suggestion is the letter was written to Jewish Christians who lived in a Gentile society, perhaps in Asia Minor or Egypt.[8]

2. Jude's description of these believers highlights three doctrinal truths that pertain to all believers' salvation.

   a. We are "called," which is a favorite New Testament term for followers of Christ, referring to the fact we are not saved by our own merits or actions but solely as a result of God's grace in choosing or calling us. We cannot be saved unless God first chooses us. Jesus explained it this way: "No one can come to me unless the Father who sent me draws him ..." (John 6:44).

   b. We are "loved *in* God the Father." Some translations, including older versions of the NIV, read "loved *by* God the Father" (CSB), but the Greek preposition *en* is best translated "in" rather than "by." Thus, the focus of the phrase is more on the believer's *position* in God's love rather than God as the *agent* of the love. In other words, not only does God love us, but His love for us is so intimate we are "embraced and enfolded by his love."[9]

   c. We are "kept *for* Jesus Christ." Again, some translations of the Bible translate this phrase as "kept *by* Jesus Christ." Jude's focus, however, was not on *who* keeps us, but on *why* we are kept. Such a focus emphasizes the security and permanence of our salvation. In other words, our salvation is secure until Christ's return, and our salvation is preserved, not for our sake, but for the glory of Jesus Christ.[10]

3. Jude issued a standard greeting and blessing in verse 2, praying for his readers to be filled with "mercy, peace and love ... in abundance." Obviously, as believers they—and we—already possess these blessings. Thus, Jude's prayer was not so much about obtaining the

blessings but that believers would recognize they already have them and would begin to utilize them in their daily lives.[11]

D. **Date.** Determining when the book of Jude was written has generated a lot of debate among commentators, with dates ranging from 40 A.D. to 120 A.D. For those who believe the letter was written by Jude, the dates range generally from 40 A.D. to 80 A.D., depending on how commentators view the relationship between Jude and 2 Peter.

1. The issue of the relationship between Jude and 2 Peter arises because of the similarity between Jude 4-19 and 2 Peter 2:1-3:3. Scholars have proposed three primary theories to explain why the wording of these two passages is so similar: (a) Peter borrowed from Jude, which means Jude was written first, (b) Jude borrowed from Peter, which means Peter was written first, or (c) Peter and Jude borrowed from a third source. Which theory is true is insignificant for any reason other than dating the letters.[12]

    a. We know 2 Peter had to have been written before Peter was killed by Nero around 64-66 A.D. If Jude borrowed from 2 Peter, then Jude's letter must be dated sometime between the mid-60s and 80 A.D.[13]

    b. If Peter borrowed from Jude, then Jude was written first and could be dated between A.D. 40 and 65.[14] More likely, it would have been written close to the same time as 2 Peter in the early- to mid-60s A.D.

    c. If Peter and Jude used a common source, then 2 Peter and Jude would likely have been written around the same time somewhere in the early- to mid-60s A.D.[15]

2. The preponderance of the evidence best supports the view that 2 Peter was written earlier than Jude. In such a case, the most likely date for the book of Jude falls sometime between 65 and 80 A.D.

Bible Study Notes on Jude

A Quick Glance at Jude

WHO was the author?	**WHO were the recipients?**
Jude, the brother of Jesus and James (v. 1)	Believers: "Those who have been called" (v. 1)
WHEN was the letter written?	**WHY was the letter written?**
Probably sometime between 65 and 80 A.D.	To warn his readers about false teachers who taught that grace gives believers a license to sin and who denied Jesus (v. 4)
WHAT is the basic outline of the letter?	**WHAT is the major theme of the letter?**
Warnings about False Teachers (vv. 1-16) Exhortations to Believers (vv. 17-25)	Contending earnestly for the faith

A One-Sentence Summary of the Letter

Jude describes the deceptive character of those who are false teachers and encourages believers to contend for the faith.

Jude 1-2

Questions for Personal Reflection or Group Discussion

1. *Jude 1a:* Why did Jude identify himself as "a servant of Jesus Christ" rather than as a brother of Jesus Christ?

2. *Jude 1a:* What is the significance of the phrase "servant of Jesus Christ" for understanding what Jude and other early church leaders believed about who Jesus is?

3. *Jude 1b:* What three characteristics did Jude use to describe the believers to whom he wrote? How do these characteristics apply to you?

4. *Jude 1b:* What does it mean that believers have been "called"? How does knowing that God "called" you to follow Him affect your relationship with Him?

5. *Jude 1b:* What does being loved "*in* God the Father" add to the fact that you are loved *by* God the Father?

6. *Jude 1b:* What is the difference between being "kept *for* Jesus Christ" and "being kept *by* Jesus Christ"? What is the significance of both of these phrases regarding your salvation?

7. *Jude 2:* What was Jude's prayer for his readers? How does the prayer apply to you?

Chapter II

Warnings about False Teachers
Jude 3-16

A. *Contending for the Faith* **(Jude 3-4)**

1. At first, Jude wanted to write an encouraging letter to the believers about salvation, perhaps a discussion of the general doctrinal elements of salvation such as man's sinful nature, God's grace, and Christ's sacrifice for us (v. 3a). Instead, something happened or he learned about some problems in the church or churches he was writing to that caused him to change the topic to a more pressing and urgent matter: the need for the believers to "contend for the faith" (v. 3b) against those who had infiltrated the church with false and ungodly teachings and lifestyles (v. 4).

    a. Jude specifically urged his readers to "contend for the faith that was once for all entrusted to God's holy people" (v. 3b). This phrase is packed with several significant terms and phrases.

    > **What does it mean to "contend for the faith"?**

    (1) The Greek word for "contend" (*epagonizesthai*) is a strong and forceful word used more in an athletic sense than in a warfare sense. It literally

means to struggle or put forth a great effort for something.[1] It does not simply refer to resisting attacks against our faith but earnestly and vigorously fighting for the truth of our faith.[2]

(a) In other words, Jude exhorted believers to be on the offense rather than the defense. We are to be "contenders" for our faith, not merely spectators, which means we must actively promote the gospel and its truth by our lives, words, and actions.[3]

(b) Jude described the means by which we do this in verses 17-23, but before getting to that, he explained in verses 5-16 the character of those who were trying to pollute and confuse the true doctrines of the faith and the outcome they could expect. This description was not for the purpose of encouraging believers to verbally accost false teachers but to awaken believers to the reality and danger of the situation they faced.[4]

(2) As believers, we are to contend for the "faith that was once for all entrusted to God's holy people" (v. 3b).

(a) Often, the word "faith," when used in the New Testament, speaks of the act of believing in the truth. But Jude used it here in a more general sense, referring to the body of truth that constitutes the basic, orthodox doctrines and beliefs of Christianity, particularly those doctrines relating to Jesus Christ.[5]

(b) Jude described the faith as "once for all entrusted to God's holy people" (v.3b). "Once for all" highlights the fact that our faith (i.e., true Christian doctrine, including, in particular, the message of salvation by grace through faith only in Jesus Christ) will not change. The truths and doctrines of our faith have been delivered in their final and unalterable state.[6]

(c) The truths of our faith have also been "entrusted to God's holy people" (v. 3b). Other versions say "delivered to the saints" (ESV) or "handed down to the saints" (NASB), both of which may indicate the meaning more fully. The body of Christian doctrine has been handed down to us from the teachings of Jesus Christ to His apostles who taught them to the early believers who passed them on to the next generation and from generation to generation thereafter in a living chain of believers that connects us today all the way back to Jesus Christ.[7]

> i. We have not discovered these truths ourselves. They have been passed down to us, and no matter how hard the world tries to diminish and discredit what we believe by calling it strange or outdated, we do not hold to our faith alone. That is why it is important we understand what we believe from a biblical standpoint and not from a contemporary or cultural viewpoint.

ii. In addition, the faith has been "entrusted" to believers. It has been passed down through the Church, where those truths are to be preserved and proclaimed. We remain part of the chain and are obligated to pass on the truths of our faith to the next generation in an accurate and uncorrupted manner.[8]

b. Jude's willingness to change the purpose of his letter from an encouraging study of the meaning of salvation to an urgent call to spiritual arms is a good example of the fact that sometimes we need to hear the negative and the difficult. Even though he wanted to write an uplifting letter, he was "compelled" to write on a more pressing matter: the denunciation of false teaching and the exhortation for believers to stand strong—to "contend"—for their faith. His letter did not end up being a "feel good" letter, but it is an essential letter for strengthening those who follow Jesus Christ.

2. The reason for Jude's change of topics in order to urge his readers to "contend for the faith" was due to an infiltration of "ungodly" men who had "secretly slipped in among" the churches and begun to spread false teachings about the grace of God and Jesus Christ (v. 4).

a. Jude called them "certain individuals" (v. 4a), which Jude may have used in a contemptuous manner. They were likely itinerant teachers who travelled among the churches, teaching and preaching their false doctrines. They appeared as loving and true teachers, but they were actually "ungodly people" (v. 4b) who did not share in true Christian beliefs about God or Jesus Christ. They were the perfect depiction of wolves in sheep's clothing.

b. These men "secretly slipped in among" the believers, or as other versions put it, they "crept in unnoticed" (ESV, NASB), came "in by stealth" (CSB), "sneaked in among" them (CEV), "smuggled themselves in" (Kelly), and "wormed their way in" (REB). These different translations highlight the fact that the false teachers infiltrated the churches with a conscious intent of changing the believers' views and beliefs about biblical teachings and doctrines.[9] One commentator calls them "spiritual terrorists."[10]

(1) The situation Jude addressed is similar to that faced by churches today. The Christian church has always faced opposition from many false teachers outside of the Church who spread lies and deceit about Christ and Christians. But, in reality, the greatest threats to the Church are those who creep inside it to mislead believers with false doctrines and deceptive teachings. As Pastor John MacArthur explains, outside attacks typically unite a church while attacks within the church by false teachers often divide and confuse it.[11]

> **Are there people in the church today who are similar to these false teachers?**

(2) MacArthur further says that, when false teachers arise within a church, they begin to destroy the church's real purposes for its existence, such as to worship God, minister to others, evangelize the lost, and provide genuine fellowship

among the believers. False doctrines take over as the church begins to practice and favor cultural norms rather than biblical truths. These false teachers come in the forms of authors, radio and television personalities, college and seminary professors, preachers, and other leaders in the church. It is one of Satan's most effective tactics to disguise a false teacher as a messenger of truth.[12]

c. Jude said these people were condemned and their "condemnation was written about long ago" (v. 4a). This is a difficult phrase to understand, and commentators have reached different conclusions about its meaning. But Jude's further description of these men in verses 5-7 suggests he was saying that the consequence for deceiving people with false teachings, especially when the deception is aimed at believers, is condemnation as illustrated by several stories told in the Old Testament.[13]

d. Their false teachings fell into two categories:

(1) *Perverting God's Grace.* The first type of false teachings they espoused "perverted" God's grace into a "license for immorality" (v. 4b). These spiritual charlatans taught that, since believers are saved by the grace of God and totally forgiven, they then became free to live without moral restraint.[14]

> **The viewpoint that God's grace relieves Christians from a duty to obey the moral laws is called "antinomianism."**

(a) The Greek word for "immorality" that Jude used to describe the lifestyle these false teachers advocated (*aselgeia*) is one that typically refers to sexual indulgence.[15] Different translations call it "sensuality" (ESV, CSB), "licentiousness" (NASB), and "lewdness" (NKJV).

(b) The libertine teachings of the false teachers remains a common belief among many people in the church today, although it may not be voiced so blatantly. Such a view explains why many people in the church today live together outside of marriage yet fail to see such a choice as being inconsistent with their professed Christian faith, and why many churches and denominations are rapidly caving in to the culture's views on homosexuality, gender identity, and other sexual sins.

(2) *Denying Jesus Christ.* The second type of false teaching were those that "deny Jesus Christ" and His sovereignty and lordship (v. 4). In other words, by living flagrantly in disobedience to the teachings of Christ, they denied that Jesus was sovereign (i.e., the supreme authority) and Lord (i.e., in charge of their lives). As Jesus put it, "Why do you call me, 'Lord, Lord,' and do not do what I say" (Luke 6:46). Thus, when we choose to disobey Christ's commands, we are in essence denying His sovereignty and lordship over our lives and subjecting ourselves to a different master.

(a) William Barclay lists four ways we deny Christ.[16]

   i. We deny Him by renouncing Him when we are in the midst of persecution for our beliefs.

   ii. We deny Him by ignoring Him when it is more convenient for us to do so.

   iii. We deny Him by living differently than what He has commanded.

   iv. We deny Him by believing in false ideas and teachings about Him.

(b) A good example of denying Christ by believing false teachings was the development of various Gnostic ideas about Jesus that developed in the late first and early second centuries. The Apostle John addressed an early version of these false teachings about Christ in his first epistle when he said, "Who is the liar? It is whoever denies that Jesus is the Christ. Such a person is the antichrist—denying the Father and the Son. No one who denies the Son has the Father; whoever acknowledges the Son has the Father also" (1 John 2:22-23).

   i. One group of false teachers John faced were those who apparently denied the incarnation of Jesus Christ. This teaching may have come from a group called Docetics, who taught that flesh was evil and, therefore, it was impossible for God to take on a fleshly nature. John said, however, "This is how you can recognize the Spirit of God: Every spirit that acknowledges that Jesus Christ has come in the flesh is from God, but every spirit that does not acknowledge Jesus is not from God" (1 John 4:2-3).

ii. A second group of false teachers John encountered were the followers of Cerinthus, who distinguished between the divine Christ and the human Jesus, claiming that Jesus actually was not divine until His baptism and that the Christ-spirit left Him immediately prior to His death. John responded to this claim when he explained that Jesus is "the one who came by water and blood …. He did not come by water only, but by water and blood" (1 John 5:6).

iii. These two views still exist today in various forms.

(A) Different religions, cults, and religious sects try to water down exactly who Jesus is because by doing so they water down His demands and His commands. As a result, it becomes easier to ignore those parts of His words we do not want to obey because, if we can lessen His position, we reduce His authority over us.

(B) However, it is not just other religions that reject who Jesus Christ is.

Based on a poll by George Barna several years ago, 44% of people who called themselves Christians agreed that Jesus sinned during His lifetime, and another 8% said they did not know if He sinned. Only 40% held a strong view that Jesus did not sin.[17] Is it possible to be a Christian and believe Jesus Christ was a sinner no different from us? Not according to Scripture, yet there are millions of people who call themselves Christians who think such a belief is an option.

(C) The biblical doctrines and truths about Christ are exactly what Jude exhorted us as believers to contend for. We live in a rapidly expanding pluralistic culture that tells us we must be tolerant of all people's beliefs and lifestyles, which really means we are expected to affirm and accept as truth all other beliefs and lifestyles. Jude, however, taught we must not have that kind of "tolerance," but instead must actively contend for *the* faith and protect the sound doctrines of the faith from such cultural opposi-

> **We live in a rapidly expanding pluralistic culture that tells us we must be tolerant of all people's beliefs and lifestyles, which really means we are expected to affirm and accept as truth all other beliefs and lifestyles. Jude, however, taught we must not have that kind of "tolerance."**

tion. As believers, Jude encouraged us to hold steadfastly to godly beliefs and conduct even in the midst of widespread ungodliness all around us.

B. *Describing the False Teachers* **(Jude 5-16).** Jude focused further on the nature and ultimate condemnation of the false teachers, using Old Testament examples of those who were condemned when they rejected God's authority and applying those examples to the false teachers (whom he referred to as "these people" each time he made the application (vv. 8, 12, 16)).

1. THEIR IMMORALITY (vv. 5-10)

    a. In verses 5-7, Jude cited three Old Testament examples of divine judgment against the ungodly. These were familiar stories in Jewish literature that Jude's readers "already know" (v. 5a), and were traditionally used to illustrate the certainty of God's judgment upon those who rejected Him.[18]

    (1) *The Example of the Israelites in the Wilderness* (v. 5). First, Jude cited God's deliverance of the Jews out of Egypt (Exodus 12-14) and their later rebellion against God when they heard the negative report of ten of the twelve spies who investigated the Promised Land. Numbers 14 tells of the people grumbling against Moses and Aaron, wishing they had died in Egypt, and plotting to stone Moses and find a new leader to take them back to Egypt (Numbers 14:1-10). God was angered at the people's unbelief and presumptuousness and was ready to destroy all of them with a plague. But He relented after

Moses prayed for them. Nevertheless, God refused to let any of them (except Joshua and Caleb, the two faithful spies) enter into the Promised Land (Numbers 14:11-20). As a result, the entire generation of Jews died in the wilderness without seeing the Promised Land—the destruction Jude referred to in verse 5 (Numbers 14:21-38).

(2) *The Example of Fallen Angels* (v. 6)

(a) Many scholars believe Jude's example in verse 6 referred to the story of fallen angels told in the nonbiblical book of 1 Enoch, a pseudepigraphal writing penned sometime between the second century B.C. and first century A.D.[19] The story, as told in 1 Enoch, explains the strange account of the "sons of God" in Genesis 6:1-4, claiming that two hundred angels who lusted after beautiful human women, led by an angel named Samjaza, descended upon earth and took wives among the women. Their offspring became great giants on earth, who continued to commit sexual sins and widespread corruption across the earth.[20]

(b) Jude used a brief play-on-words when he said these angels "did not keep their positions," so God "kept" them in chains.

(3) *The Example of Sodom and Gomorrah* (v. 7)

(a) Jude's third example was the well-known story of the destruction of Sodom and Gomorrah in Genesis 18:16-19:9. The sins of Sodom and Gomorrah that brought about their destruction included the sin of homosexuality, although Jude never directly accused the false teachers of committing the sin of homosexuality. The Greek word translated "perversion" in verse 7 means literally "went after strange flesh" (NASB), which may refer to the Sodomites' desire for sex with angels (in contrast to the previous story of angels desiring sex with humans). Jude's purpose in these last two examples, then, is to point out the violation by the false teachers of God's created order, which is consistent with Jude's earlier charge that the false teachers denied Jesus as Sovereign and Lord.

(b) The issue of homosexuality in our culture is a hot topic and has created significant tension between modern culture and Christian teachings. The culture calls those who consider homosexuality sin "homophobic" and "hateful." As a result, many Christians, being intimidated by such name-calling, have reevaluated their beliefs about homosexuality and now claim the Bible does not consider it sinful conduct.[21]

  i. Nevertheless, while many try to explain away the Scriptures on the subject, there really is no valid way to interpret Scripture's teaching other than as a prohibition against homosexuality. The efforts to deny the clear teaching of Scripture about homosexuality are merely attempts to change the meaning of Scripture so that it supports current societal behaviors and values rather than let the Bible define what constitutes correct behaviors and values. As believers, regardless of how violently the culture opposes us, we must let the Bible, not culture, determine our values and beliefs.

ii. Although believers must stand strong on the teachings of Scripture about homosexuality, we must also be careful that we engage the world in a manner that does not turn them away from the truth. As Commentator Douglas Moo explains, believers must proclaim the truth of Scripture in the right spirit. While opponents of the Scripture's teachings on this issue blindly and automatically accuse those who stand by Scripture as being "homophobic," believers must be careful they do not approach the subject with a homophobic intent and attitude. In other words, we must not speak against homosexuality out of hatred or disgust. Instead, we should declare the truth of Scripture because we have been called to "contend for the faith" and because we sincerely and lovingly desire those who are homosexuals to recognize and accept the true teachings of Scripture.[22]

b. Beginning in verse 8, Jude applied the three examples to the false teachers. Apparently the false teachers claimed they received their teachings from prophetic visions and dreams, which prompted Jude to mention sarcastically that they relied on "the strength of their dreams" (v. 8a) to lead them into their rebellion and lies.[23] Other commentators, though, understand Jude's reference to dreams as meaning the false teachers were out of touch with reality, "dreaming" they were free to do as they pleased in life, and unaware of God's consequences for such conduct.[24] Whichever meaning Jude intended, his clear intent was to show how the false teachers committed the same sins as those who were judged in the examples he cited. He listed four specific sins the false teachers committed.

(1) *Sexual Immorality* ("pollute their own bodies") (v. 8a). Other translations say, "defile the flesh" (ESV, NASB, CSB). The term most likely refers to sexual sins, possibly including homosexuality based upon the example of Sodom and Gomorrah.

(2) *Rebelliousness* ("reject authority") (v. 8b). Based upon Jude's earlier reference of denying Christ as Sovereign and Lord (v. 4), Jude probably referred to the false teachers' rejection of God's authority in their lives, as opposed to the authority of any church or secular leader.

(3) *Misplaced Confidence in Their Own Authority* ("heap abuse on celestial beings") (v. 8c). It is not exactly clear what Jude meant by this statement or in what manner the false teachers abused these heavenly beings. The word translated by the NIV as "heap abuse on" typically means to "blaspheme" (ESV), "slander" (CSB),

or "revile" (NASB). The object of the blasphemy, though, is not God but angels.

(a) Jude referred to the example of how the Archangel Michael refused to speak slanderously of Satan (based on a story found in the apocryphal book *The Assumption of Moses*) (v. 9).[25] The lesson of the story is *not*, as some erroneously conclude, that Michael treated Satan with respect and therefore we should, too. Instead, the story emphasizes that Michael's denunciation of Satan was based on the Lord's authority, not in reliance upon his own self-assumed authority.

(b) While we are uncertain how the false teachers blasphemed angels, the point Jude was making is that they claimed their own authority over the celestial beings. They usurped the authority of God and tried to be a law unto themselves, thinking they had the right or power to condemn angels by their own right. Jude refuted their ability to do so with the story of Michael's and Satan's dispute over Moses' body.

(c) For us today, this is a reminder that we too are not a law unto ourselves. In our culture, we express it as "having our own truths." Truth, however, is defined by God, and it remains truth regardless of how culture tries to change it. There are no individual "truths"

> **Truth is defined by God, and it remains truth regardless of how culture tries to change it. There are no individual "truths."**

that each of us can adopt for our own selfish purposes.

(4) *Ignorance of the Truth* (v. 10). The false teachers spoke against the truths of Scripture because they did not understand those truths. Instead,

---

The Pseudepigrapha

1 Enoch and *The Assumption of Moses* are part of a body of literature called the Old Testament Pseudepigrapha, a collection of Jewish writings composed generally between 200 B.C. and 200 A.D. The word "pseudepigrapha" literally means "false title" and refers to the fact that many of the writings falsely claim to have been authored by various Old Testament characters.

None of the pseudepigraphal writings were considered to be inspired and thus were never included in the canon of the Bible. Nevertheless many of them were still known and read by early Christians. Although they are not biblical sources, they provide helpful insights into the lives and theology of intertestamental Judaism.

1 Enoch consists of five sections that include stories of fallen angels, parables of judgment and eschatology, discussions on astronomy, prophecies of then-future events from the Flood to the Maccabean Revolt, and teachings about the suffering of the righteous.

Only portions of *The Assumption of Moses* still exist today. It is sometimes referred to as *The Testament of Moses*. The writing contains alleged prophecies spoken to Joshua by Moses shortly before Moses's death. The prophecies cover Jewish history through the intertestamental period and includes prophecies about Herod the Great and the coming of the Messiah.

they taught only what they did understand, the base and vile things that turned out to be the very things that would destroy them, i.e., sin, rebelliousness, licentiousness, etc.

2. THEIR DECEPTION OF OTHERS (vv. 11-13)

   a. Jude was not yet finished describing the false teachers. In verses 5-10, he focused on their immoral and sinful *conduct*. In verses 11-13, the examples and description he used focused more on the falseness of their *teachings*. In verse 11, Jude declared "woe" upon them and cited three Old Testament examples, all of which were traditional Jewish stories of evildoers, in order to convey why their future was one of destruction and judgment:

      (1) *The Example of Cain* (v. 11a)

         (a) The story of Cain's murder of Abel is told in Genesis 4:1-15 and identifies Cain, not only as one who rejected God's authority, but also as a murderer and sinner. Jewish tradition, which was probably very well known to Jude and his readers, depicted Cain as much more than simply a murderer. He was the archetypical sinner and the prototype for hatred and envy.[26] The early Jewish historian, Josephus, described Cain as wicked, greedy, scheming, and violent.[27] The Apostle John referred to Cain as belonging to "the evil one" (1 John 3:12).

         (b) Jude said the false teachers had "taken the way" of Cain by imitating his wickedness and greed, thus exposing the insincerity of their ministry.

(2) *The Example of Balaam* (v. 11b)
 (a) The story of Balaam is told in Numbers 22-24. When the Israelites attempted to pass through the land of Moab on their way to the Promised Land, Balak, the Moabite king, sought to hire Balaam, an apparent mystic of some sort, to curse the Israelites and thus allow the Moabites to defeat them in battle. Balaam, however, after being clearly warned by God, refused to declare a curse against the Israelites.
  i. Although Balaam never voiced the curse Balak wanted, he advised Balak regarding other ways he could defeat the Israelites. Balaam encouraged Balak to entice the Israelites with Moabite women, drawing them into sexual immorality and eventually Baal worship and idolatry (Revelation 2:14; Numbers 31:16). According to Numbers 25:1-3, "While Israel was staying in Shittim, the men began to indulge in sexual immorality with Moabite women, who invited them to the sacrifices to their gods. The people ate the sacrificial meal and bowed down before these gods. So Israel yoked themselves to the Baal of Peor. And the Lord's anger burned against them." As a result, God brought a plague upon Israel and 24,000 people died (Numbers 25:9).
  ii. Consequently, Jewish tradition treats Balaam as the villain and enemy of

God's people who advised Balak to entice the people into sinning against God, all in return for money.[28]

(b) Jude compared the false teachers to Balaam by describing them as people who taught false teachings primarily for monetary gain, declaring that "they have rushed for profit into Balaam's error" (v. 11b). But the comparison was not only that they sinned for the sake of gain but that they also taught others to sin for the sake of gain.

(3) *The Example of Korah* (v. 11c)

(a) Jude's third example is that of Korah, who, out of envy for Moses' position, led a rebellion against Moses, enticing two hundred fifty other men to join him in opposition against Moses' leadership (Numbers 16:1-3). In the end, God destroyed Korah and the other leaders of the rebellion by opening up the ground, swallowing them into it, and destroying their two hundred fifty followers with fire from the sky (Numbers 16:31-35; Numbers 26:9-10; Psalm 106:16-18).

(b) To the Jews, Korah was the classic example of a "lawless heretic" who defied authority.[29] Jude likened the false teachers to Korah as well and declared the certainty of their ultimate destruction (v. 11c).

b. Jude made further application of these examples to the false teachers in a series of six blistering metaphors, again signaling the application with the words "these people" (v. 12).

Jude 3-16

(1) *Hidden Reefs* (v. 12a)

(a) Jude said the false teachers participated in the church's "love feasts," which were fellowship meals that often included communion as well.[30] There they spread their false teachings "without the slightest qualm" in what they were doing.

(b) The NIV reads, "These people are blemishes at your love feasts," but the better translation is "hidden reefs" rather than "blemishes" (ESV, NASB). The Greek word translated "blemishes" (*spilades*) means "hidden rocks," referring to rocks that are barely submerged close to shore and are dangerous to the ships that sail nearby.[31] Jude's point was that the false teachers were dangerous to the believers and could potentially "shipwreck" their faith. Thus, Jude warned his readers to steer clear of them and avoid close association with them.[32] This is also the lesson learned from the example of Korah.

(2) *Selfish Shepherds* (v. 12b)

(a) By eating with the people, the false teachers pretended to be shepherds who cared for them. But, like Balaam, the false teachers only cared for themselves.

(b) Jude's shepherd metaphor is reminiscent of Ezekiel's prophecy in Ezekiel 34: "Woe to you shepherds of Israel who only take care of yourselves! Should not shepherds take care of the flock? You eat the curds, clothe yourselves with the wool and slaughter the choice animals, but you do not take care of the flock. You have not strengthened the weak or healed the sick or bound up the injured. You have not brought back the strays or searched for the lost. You have ruled them harshly and brutally. ... Therefore, you shepherds, hear the word of the Lord: This is what the Sovereign Lord says: I am against the shepherds and will hold them accountable for my flock" (Ezekiel 34:2-4, 9-10).

(3) *Rainless Clouds* (v. 12c). Jude compared the false teachers to "clouds without rain"—that is, teachers who made empty promises and provided no benefit to the people.[33] His description

Jude's Metaphors for False Teachers (v. 12-13)	
Hidden Reefs	Teachers who can "shipwreck" the faith of believers
Selfish Shepherds	Teachers who care only for their own self interests
Rainless Clouds	Teachers who make empty promises and provide no benefit to others
Fruitless Trees	Teachers who bear no fruit and deliver nothing but disappointment
Foaming Waves	Teachers whose teachings and lives reveal only their shame and filth
Wandering Stars	Teachers who fail to follow God's truths and are doomed to the "blackest darkness"

was similar to Solomon's wise saying in Proverbs 25:14: "Like clouds and wind without rain is one who boasts of gifts never given."

(4) *Fruitless Trees* (v. 12d)

(a) In a similar metaphor to that of the rainless clouds, Jude compared the false teachers to dormant trees that lacked fruit. Being "autumn trees," they were bare and leafless, delivering nothing but disappointment.

(b) Jude added a reference to the judgment the false teachers would face by speaking of the trees being "twice dead," once by their fruitlessness and second when they were uprooted. This is most likely an allusion to the second death nonbelievers will face in the judgment.[34]

(5) *Foaming Waves* (v. 13a). Jude's next comparison may have been based on Isaiah 57:20, which says, "The wicked are like the tossing sea, which cannot rest, whose waves cast up mire and mud." He compared the false teachers to the churning sea that washed up filth and debris on the shore. Their teachings and lives only resulted in revealing "their shame" and their dirty works.

(6) *Wandering Stars* (v. 13b). Jude's final metaphor likened the false teachers to "wandering stars," which may have been a metaphor he picked up again from the book of 1 Enoch, which compares fallen angels to falling stars.[35] Some commentators, though, believe Jude was speaking of comets (i.e., shooting stars) or planets, which

the ancient people believed were stars that failed to follow their God-ordained orbit.[36] Regardless of which meaning Jude intended, the end result was that the false teachers were doomed to the "blackest darkness."

3. THEIR ARROGANCE (vv. 14-16)

   a. Jude's tirade against the false teachers reached a climax with a final quotation from 1 Enoch 1:9 that highlighted the return of Jesus Christ on the Day of Judgment when He will return to earth to condemn ungodly people (vv. 14-15).[37] The repetition of "ungodly" in the quotation is probably the reason Jude chose the quotation because it so forcefully emphasized the point he was making about the depraved teachings and lifestyles of the false teachers.[38]

   b. Jude again made application of the prophecies of Enoch with the phrase "these people" (v. 16). He had already spoken of the "ungodly acts" of the false teachers in the previous verses. In verse 16, he focused more on the last part of Enoch's prophecy about the ungodly ones who speak "defiant words" (v. 15) or "harsh things" (ESV, NASB, CSB) against God, characterizing the words the false teachers spoke with five descriptions.

      (1) *Grumbling* (v. 16a). The false teachers were "grumblers" who complained about God and the restrictions He placed upon His followers by His moral laws and ethics. Their grumbling was similar to the conduct of Korah, who resisted God's authority.[39]

      (2) *Fault-Finding* (v. 16b). Jude called the false teachers "faultfinders" or "malcontents" (ESV).

They were discontented with submitting themselves to God and blamed God for any unhappiness or dissatisfaction they experienced.

(3) *Rebelling* (v. 16c). The false teachers "[followed] their own evil desires." They rebelled against God's authority and chose to do as they wanted to do without restrictions. They followed the idea of "doing what felt good to them," a popular motto of our day and culture.

(4) *Boasting* (v. 16d). The Greek word for "boast" (*huperongkos*) conveys more than mere boasting, but literally means "bulging over" and refers to "big words and arrogant speech."[40] The NKJV translates the phrase, "They mouth great swelling words." Jude accused the false teachers of being arrogant and contemptuous toward God and His commandments, rejecting His moral authority and boastfully claiming their own authority to live as they choose.

(5) *Flattering* (v. 16e). Jude also criticized the false teachers as being flatterers "for their own advantage." The Greek word for "flatter" (*thaumazontes*) referred to showing favoritism. The false teachers were sycophants, teaching what their listeners wanted to hear, especially in order to please their benefactors who provided them the money and resources they depended on for their living.[41]

Bible Study Notes on Jude

Questions for Personal Reflection or Group Discussion

1. *Jude 3:* What does it mean to "contend for the faith"? Have you ever faced a time when you had to "contend for the faith"?

2. *Jude 3:* What is the importance of our faith having been "once for all entrusted to God's holy people"?

    a. How does the term "once for all" impact the finality of our faith? Compare the term to its other uses in Romans 6:10, Hebrews 7:27, 9:12, 9:26, 10:2, 10:10, and 1 Peter 3:18.

    b. In what way are you a part of the "living chain" that is connected all the way back to Jesus Christ, and what responsibilities does that mean you have?

3. *Jude 3-4:* Jude wrote the letter because he was concerned about "certain individuals" who had infiltrated the churches, spreading false teachings. What were the false teachings being spread by these individuals? Do these false teachings still exist today?

4. *Jude 5-10:* What three examples did Jude use to describe the certain condemnation of these false teachers? What kind of lifestyle did the false teachers live that brought such condemnation upon them?

    a. *Jude 8-9:* Why were Michael and Satan disputing over the body of Moses? What is the meaning of the story of Michael's dispute with Satan over Moses' body?

b. Some people believe the Michael-Satan dispute teaches that we should never speak out in judgment against others. Is that a correct interpretation of the meaning of the story? If so, does Jude violate such a principle by his harsh words of condemnation against the false teachers?

5. *Jude 11-13:* What three examples did Jude use to describe the false teachings of these individuals? What six things did Jude compare their false teachings to?

6. *Jude 14-16:* Jude used a quote from a nonbiblical source to highlight the ungodliness of the false teachers. What ungodly action did Jude specifically accuse the false teachers of committing?

7. On a side note, does Jude's use of nonbiblical sources create any issues with regard to whether the biblical canon is complete? For instance, does Jude's use of quotations and material from 1 Enoch and *The Assumption of Moses* mean that he thought they are inspired Scripture that should be included in the Bible?

8. Is there any similarity between the false teachers and teachings that Jude's readers faced and what we face today?

9. What are some examples of false teachings in the church today?

Chapter III
Strategies for Contending for the Faith
Jude 17-23

A. *Remember What God's Word Says* **(Jude 17-19)**. In these verses, Jude returned to the language and primary topic of verse 3, focusing now on his readers whom he called his "dear friends" (NIV, CSB) or "beloved" (ESV, NASB). He started in verse 3 with a call to his readers to "contend for the faith." Then in verses 5-16, he explained the reason they must contend for the faith against the intrusion of false teachers among them and exposed the nature and character of the false teachers. Beginning in verse 17, he provided believers with a three-fold strategy for how to contend for the faith against false teachers.

1. The first strategy we must use to deal with false teachings is to *remember what God's Word says*, or as Jude put it, "remember what the apostles of our Lord Jesus Christ foretold" (v. 17). Jude cited the teachings of the apostles that foretold about "scoffers" in "the last times" who would follow "their own ungodly desires" (v. 18).[1]

    a. The quotation in verse 18 is not found anywhere in the New Testament. It is likely that Jude paraphrased or summarized the many warnings made

39

by Jesus and the apostles throughout the New Testament regarding false prophets rather than actually attempt to quote a specific passage. Doubtless, the New Testament is replete with such warnings about false prophets and teachers.[2]

b. "Scoffers" referred to people who "despise and ignore religion and morality."[3]

c. The "last times," to the New Testament Christian, referred to the time period from the incarnation of Christ until His Second Coming. The early Christians believed they were living in the last days, so the phrase is applicable to the Church Age in general.[4]

2. Jude took one last swipe at the false teachers, pointing out how they cause divisions among believers. The Greek word translated "divide" (*apodiopizontes*) literally refers to making distinctions between people. Apparently, the false teachers were elitists who claimed to be more spiritual than others because of their supposed greater insights about the truth. But Jude said, in reality, they were merely following "natural instincts" and lacked the Holy Spirit in their lives (v. 19).

3. The important point Jude made to his readers by calling them to remember what God had foretold was that none of this apostasy was a surprise to God. God knew it would happen and has as-

> **Why is it important for us to remember what God's Word says when we need to "contend for the faith" against those who misrepresent the truth?**

sured us that His will shall prevail regardless. Such a reminder gives us confidence that God is—and always has been—in control.

    a. Even today, the growing anti-Christian culture in our country is not a surprise to God. When we are reminded of that, we can avoid becoming discouraged or stressed by the godlessness of our world and recognize God is not caught off guard but remains in control—no matter what.

    b. The call to "remember" God's Word, though, is not merely an act of our minds. The word includes our will. In other words, spiritual "remembering" means recalling and applying God's Word in such a way that it affects both the way we think and the way we behave and, thus, helps us be able to better respond to false teachers and false teachings.[5]

    c. We must be on guard, watch out for false teachings, and avoid drifting from the truth of God's Word.

4. MacArthur points out that the ability to recognize false teachers and false teachings requires the ability to discern between what is false and what is true. He says such spiritual discernment is missing in churches today for six reasons.[6]

    a. *Reason #1: A decreased focus on doctrine and its importance*, which has resulted in church-goers being fed an incomplete gospel of grace only without reference to sin, holiness, or judgment. Without an emphasis on biblical doctrine, churches tend to lead people into compromising solid theological doctrine with secular ideas and believing that the church's ministries are solely for their satisfaction, pleasure, and comfort. Consequently, they are unable to identify false teaching, much less know how to cope with it.

b. *Reason #2: The replacement of absolute truth with moral relativism.* An increasing number of Christians today are taking the position, along with a vast majority of the world's non-Christians, that what is morally acceptable behavior depends primarily on our circumstances and feelings. People are making decisions about morality based on the philosophies of "if it feels good, do it," or "everyone else is doing it," or "as long as it doesn't hurt anyone else, it's okay." The Word of God is not even taken into consideration in the choices they make.

This slide into relativism is applicable, not only with respect to moral decision-making, but in other areas as well, all holding to the idea that there is no absolute truth. Christians without doctrinal grounding are slowly buying into the world's idea that everybody's beliefs are equally legitimate and true. Such a viewpoint is inconsistent with the Bible's clear teachings of right and wrong and truth and error.

c. *Reason #3: The church's obsession with image over Scripture.* In other words, the local church often seeks to reach the world by becoming like the world, mistaking any increased attendance with effective gospel outreach.

d. *Reason #4: The failure to properly study and interpret the Scriptures.* MacArthur attributes much of the doctrinal errors in churches to "pastoral laziness, exegetical sloppiness, and a general attitude of indifference to God's Word."

e. *Reason #5: The neglect of the church to exercise church discipline.*

f. *Reason #6: A widespread lack of spiritual maturity among the church's members.* Without the teaching of sound doctrine, churches become filled with people whose knowledge of Scripture is shallow and whose view of God is incomplete and incorrect.

B. ***Strengthen Your Spiritual Walk (Jude 20-21).***[7] The second strategy Jude mentioned for contending for the faith and combatting false teachers is to *strengthen your spiritual walk* by making sure your faith is secure and growing. One pastor said, "The best thing believers can do to withstand the malady [of apostasy] is to develop their own spiritual immunological resources."[8] Jude outlined four ways we can do that:

Strategy #2

1. BUILD YOURSELF UP IN THE FAITH (v. 20a). Using construction terminology, Jude exhorted his readers to be about "building yourselves up on your most holy faith" (v. 20a NASB).[9]

   a. The context suggests Jude spoke of building one another up in the Church by encouraging and strengthening one another so as to ensure the full body of believers is strong enough to withstand the false teachings that batter and penetrate it.[10]

      (1) This is an important reminder of how essential the church is for our own spiritual walk and growth. Becoming lax or inconsistent in our church attendance and participation weakens us spiritually in the long run and opens us up to false teachings.

(2) However, even though the exhortation to be built up may best apply to a corporate setting, it results in the strengthening of each individual in the local church. In other words, each believer has a responsibility to ensure his spiritual walk and growth remains constantly "under construction" and is being built up and strengthened through his daily experiences with God. Thus, we are not only responsible for ensuring the body of Christ is growing and becoming stronger, we are also responsible for our own individual growth by doing that which helps us mature in our walk with the Lord. Attending and serving in a local church is an essential part of that process.

b. Our spiritual growth must be grounded upon the foundation of our "most holy faith."

(1) As he did in verse 3, Jude used this term to refer to the doctrinal and ethical core of Christianity (as opposed to merely our inner beliefs and convictions).[11]

(2) It is, therefore, essential that we learn and understand what the basic doctrines of our faith are. We cannot let our desire for the Church to be relevant in the world mislead us into following the fads and values of the culture. We must remember that the truths of God are always relevant, even if they are unpopular, because the truths of God, not today's popular crazes or causes, are what will change hearts and minds.

2. PRAY IN THE HOLY SPIRIT (v. 20b). The second way we ensure our faith is growing and being strengthened is

by praying. In particular, we must be sure we are praying "in the Holy Spirit."

   a. In other words, we must approach prayer with a desire to be in harmony with God, submitted to His will in all things we desire, and filled with the Holy Spirit.[12] It means the Holy Spirit should be intimately involved in our prayers, inspiring and guiding what we say. It is this type of prayer that distinguishes believers' prayers from the prayers of others who do not know the true God.

   b. T.W. Hunt says prayer should not be done with a "mindless spirit nor spiritless mind" but with a mind that is controlled by the Holy Spirit.[13]

3. KEEP IN GOD'S LOVE (v. 21a). The third way we ensure our faith is growing and being strengthened is by keeping ourselves in the sphere or realm of God's love and blessing. Jesus spoke of it as remaining or abiding in His love, and He explained we do that by obeying His commands. In John 15:9-10, Jesus said, "As the Father has loved me, so have I loved you. Now remain in my love. *If you keep my commands, you will remain in my love*, just as I have kept my Father's commands and remain in his love" (emphasis added).

4. WAIT EXPECTANTLY FOR GOD'S RETURN (v. 21b). The fourth way to strengthen our spiritual walk is to focus on Christ's future return. To "wait for the mercy of the Lord" was a traditional term for expressing the Christian hope of Jesus Christ's return.[14] We strengthen our walks by maintaining an eager expectation and hope for Christ's return at which time He will deliver His people into a victorious "eternal life," as opposed to the ulti-

mate defeat and death the false teachers offered through their deceptive messages.

C. *Engage Those Who Are Misled* **(Jude 22-23).**[15] The third strategy for contending for the faith is to *actively engage those who are misled or misleading others* by showing them mercy and the truth. This is such an important point for us today. Believers must be able to contend for the faith in a merciful and humble way, learning to "contend without being contentious," and "without condemning, demonizing, or pretending to be superior to those who hold" unbiblical views or practice unbiblical lifestyles.[16] How do we do this?

Strategy #3

1. BE MERCIFUL TO THE DOUBTERS (v. 22)

   a. The first group Jude mentioned were "those who doubt." These are the ones who were being swayed by the false teachers but were not yet fully convinced.[17] They are the ones who are confused by false teachers and their teachings, uncertain what to do or believe.

   b. With this group, Jude said to "be merciful." In other words, we need to be compassionate and patient with them, listening to their concerns and doubts, and gently nudging them back toward the correct path of truth and sound doctrine.[18]

2. RESCUE THE DECEIVED (v. 23a)

   a. The second group Jude mentioned were those who had already gone further down the path of apostasy. They are the ones who have already been deceived by the false teachers and are counted among their followers.[19]

b. Jude used stronger words for how we must deal with this group, urging believers to "save" them "by snatching them from the fire." This implies a more aggressive and urgent approach than that used for the first group, suggesting blunt honesty and earnestness with the goal of rescuing them from disaster. Such method should still not be done in an unloving and merciless manner, but it must be done with sincerity and resolve on our part, clearly and unmistakably describing the dangerous path they have chosen.

3. BE CAUTIOUS WITH THE DECEIVERS (v. 23b)

a. The third group were the false teachers themselves—the ones who were actively teaching and deceiving others away from God and committed to continuing their deception.

b. Again, Jude said we must be merciful to these people as well, but to show such mercy, "mixed with fear." In this instance, the mercy to be shown is more akin to pity than compassion. At the same time, we are to be extremely cautious around them so that we avoid falling into their deceptions ourselves. To practice this level of caution means that we often must disassociate ourselves from them.

(1) The Apostle John called these false teachers "antichrists" and encouraged believers not to welcome them or support them in any way. He said, "If anyone comes to you and does not bring this teaching [the true gospel message], do not take them into your house or welcome them. Anyone who welcomes them shares in their wicked work" (2 John 10-11).

(2) Yet, we must be careful our separation from such people is not done out of disdain or hatred for them. Our motivation is to protect ourselves from the power of the devil working through them and to do what is necessary to ensure we do not succumb to their teachings or their lifestyles.

(3) Jude explained this response to the false teachers as hating "the clothing stained by corrupted flesh." In other words, he compared the false teachers' lifestyles of sexual immorality and libertine doctrines to "dirty underwear."[20] Our reaction to false teachings should be with the same revulsion we would have for handling the filthiness of someone's dirty underwear.

c. One issue raised by Jude's comments is the question of how much believers should associate with unbelievers. Many claim that, as believers, we cannot impact the world if we do not have non-Christian friends. They argue that Jesus "hung out" with unbelievers as well as believers, and therefore we should too.

> **Did Jesus "hang out" with sinners as part of His strategy to save them?**

(1) It is true Jesus associated with sinners, and was often criticized for it. Five particular stories in the New Testament highlight the criticism He received for being too close to sinners: the dinner He had with tax collectors after calling Matthew to follow Him (Matthew 9:11, Mark 2:16;

Luke 5:30); the labeling of Christ as a "friend of sinners" (Matthew 11:19, Luke 7:34); the sinful woman who anointed Jesus' feet and dried them with her hair (Luke 7:36-39); the setting for the parables of the lost sheep, coin, and son (Luke 15:2); and the dinner with Zacchaeus (Luke 19:7).[21]

(2) But, was Jesus, in each of these instances, simply hanging out with these tax collectors and prostitutes, hoping for a time when He would be able to witness to them and perhaps lead them to follow Him? Was that His strategy? Not at all! Pastor Kevin DeYoung explains that these stories show that sinners were drawn to Jesus where He was. He did not merely hang out with them, participating in or overlooking their immorality until such time as He could share the gospel with them. He was a friend to sinners because He welcomed them when they approached Him, seeking what He offered and repenting of their sins.[22]

(3) In other words, it is true Jesus associated with sinners, but He did so in the context of leading them to salvation. He didn't simply "hang out with guys" in order to be cool and accepted. His example was consistent with Jude's warning to us. We are not to be so separated from the world that we closet ourselves behind the walls of the church and never befriend the unsaved, but instead we must show them mercy (i.e., love and compassion) when they are genuinely seeking the truth. At the same time, we must do so

with a healthy fear in order to ensure we are not drawn into their sin.

d. Another question raised by Jude's comments is how and when to confront nonbelievers about their ungodly conduct or views, especially when such confrontation is considered hateful and intolerant and often provokes malicious and even violent reactions. Ryan Denison, a contributor to the Denison Forum blog, provides excellent insights for answering this question.[23]

> **Is there a time when believers should directly confront nonbelievers about their ungodly conduct or views?**

(1) Denison points out that Scripture provides examples of times when Christians need to speak out vocally about their faith and biblical morality. One such example was when Peter and John refused the orders of the Sanhedrin to stop speaking about Jesus Christ. In response, Peter and John told the Sanhedrin, "Which is right in God's eyes: to listen to you, or to him? You be the judges! As for us, we cannot help speaking about what we have seen and heard" (Acts 4:19-20).

(2) At other times, though, Denison says our greatest impact will be made when we simply live out our faith without any loud proclamations or vocal fanfare.

Jude 17-23

(3) It is not always easy to know which approach is the best one to take in a given situation. However, when we choose to address issues either in person or over social media, Denison offers three principles we should follow:

   (a) *Principle 1: When you speak, remember that someone is listening.* Because social media creates a feeding frenzy of comments, our words often seem to get lost in the fray. As a result, people frequently say things on social media they would never say in person or with a stridency they would never typically use, simply to make their comments more noticeable. This is not acceptable for Christians.

   i. King David prayed, "Set a guard over my mouth, Lord; keep watch over the door of my lips" (Psalm 141:3). This should be our prayer, too.

   ii. We must remember that when believers speak, they always speak on behalf of Christ. What we say and how we say it reflects upon our Lord and His Church. The Holy Spirit should guide everything we say, not only in our speech but also what we write on social media.

   (b) *Principle 2: When you speak, expect a response.* The question is what kind of response are you trying to get? Are we seeking a response from our listeners and readers that will bring them closer to God, or are we merely trying to accuse, denounce, and anger them? Denison suggests that anything we write on social media that we would not say to someone in person is more than likely a comment that does not honor God or further the gospel.

(c) *Principle 3: When you speak, do so with the hope of sharing the gospel.* We never know when God will use our words to draw someone into a conversation about Him. When we speak in such a way that people are turned off of Him and we preclude such a conversation, then we have misspoken. We must always be aware that we are, as Denison puts it, merely "one comment away from bringing shame to the Lord and his kingdom."[24]

Questions for Personal Reflection or Group Discussion

1. *Jude 17:* Why is it important to remember what God's Word teaches about the coming of false teachers when we need to "contend for the faith" against those who misrepresent the truth?

2. *Jude 17:* In order to remember God's Word we have to know and understand it to begin with. John MacArthur lists six trends that evidence the modern church member's lack of such knowledge and ability to discern what constitutes true doctrine from false. Do you agree with the trends he identifies? Based upon those trends, what practical steps do we need to take in order apply this first strategy in our lives?

3. *Jude 20-21:* What are the four things we must do in order to strengthen our own spiritual walks? Which of these four things do you need to work on the most in your own life?

    a. How important is church attendance and participation to you?

    b. What does it mean to "pray in the Holy Spirit"?

4. *Jude 22-23:* Describe the different ways we should approach those who are doubting their faith, those who have already been deceived away from the faith, and those who are actively deceiving others about the faith.

5. What do you believe is the correct response to the issue of believers "hanging out" with unbelievers? Do you agree with Pastor DeYoung's analysis of Jesus' association with sinners?

6. When must believers vocalize their opposition to ungodly laws and practices, and when is it best for believers to avoid overt opposition but simply live out their faith as an example of godliness?

Chapter IV

Doxology
Jude 24-25

A. *The Ability of God* **(Jude 24).** Jude closed his letter with a doxology of praise to God for His ability to "keep" us and "present [us] without fault."[1]

1. God's ability to "keep [us] from stumbling" (v. 24a) refers to His ability to preserve and guard us from falling into the path of mistruth and sinfulness such as the false teachers followed. God is able to preserve us from the final judgment that awaits those who reject Him.[2]

    a. The Greek word for "stumbling" (*aptaistous*) is generally used in connection with a surefooted horse and figuratively to a man who does not fall into error.[3] As the psalmist said, "He will not let your foot slip" (Psalm 121:3).

    b. The ability of God to keep us is the sole reason we can trust in the security of our salvation. If it were left up to us, we would lose our salvation. But once God redeems us, He takes the responsibility of keeping us redeemed. This is not a concept of God protecting us from sin so that we become sinless, which is not a biblical concept at all. Instead, it refers to God's protection of us from the consequences of sin and His ability to guide us to spiritual victory.

2. God is also able to "present [us] before his glorious presence without fault and with great joy" (v. 24b). Jude's statement referenced the Old Testament sacrificial system that required the Israelites to bring physically unblemished animal sacrifices to God. Jude said God is able to ensure that, when we appear before Him in heaven, we will be received "without fault," unblemished and "blameless" (ESV, NASB). This is the doctrine of justification. The salvation God provides us does not merely include the forgiveness of our sins but our entire justification before God.

   a. Justification is God's act of making and declaring us to be righteous, i.e., to be in right standing with Him. Whereas our corrupt nature is repaired by God's act of regeneration, our guilt is removed by His act of justification. Justification involves more than the forgiveness of our sins. If we were only forgiven for our sins, we would only be "morally neutral before God."[4]

   b. Since we have been justified, we are able to stand before God in a right relationship with Him, having been deemed not guilty of our sins and declared "righteous" (i.e., having completely fulfilled the requirements of the law) as though we never sinned at all—not because of anything we have done but solely because of Christ's atoning work on the cross on our behalf.

c. God is able to make this happen, which is why we will be able to stand before Him someday in heaven "with great joy."

B. *The Attributes of God* **(Jude 25).** Jude then switched to the more common form of doxology and ascribed to God great attributes.
   1. He is the "only" God. There is no god or being like Him. He is unique and the exclusive God of creation.[5]
   2. He is "our Savior." It is somewhat unusual in the New Testament to refer to God the Father as our savior rather than Jesus, but it was a traditional Jewish term for God.[6]
   3. He has "glory."[7]
      a. What is the glory of God? The glory of God is the essence and totality of God's divine attributes and characteristics. In other words, everything there is about God—who He is and what He is—constitutes His glory. It is the essence of all He is—the composite of all of His attributes and characteristics.
      b. To ascribe glory to God is a worshipful way of recognizing His magnificent character and nature. No one has glory like God. God is the only being in all of existence who possesses inherent glory. In other words, it was not given to Him. God did not do something to earn glory. He did not take it from something else. Glory already and completely belongs to Him simply by virtue of who He is.
   4. He has "majesty." Ascribing majesty to God recognizes His transcendence and greatness beyond our under-

standing. God's majesty should cause us always to respond to Him with reverence and awe.

5. He has "power" (NIV, CSB) or, according to other translations, "dominion" (ESV, NASB). Jude acknowledged God's absolute power, which ensures His ultimate victory (and, thus, ours as well).[8]

6. He has "authority." Jude praised God for His sovereignty. God is not only *able* to do as He chooses; He is *entitled* to do as He chooses because He is sovereign.[9]

7. We recognize these virtues in God "through Jesus Christ our Lord."[10]

8. God is eternal. God has possessed and continues to possess these attributes "before all ages, now and forevermore," a phrase encompassing past, present, and future.

Jude's List of God's Attributes (v. 25)	
The Only God	God is unique in His holy character and exclusively the only God
Our Savior	God is the one who saves us
Glory	The totality of God's divine attributes and characteristics are magnificent and worthy of worship and praise
Majesty	God's majesty refers to His transcendence and greatness beyond our understanding
Power	God's power is absolute and ensures His ultimate victory over His enemies
Authority	God is sovereign and entitled to do as He chooses
Eternal	God's existence has no beginning or ending. He has always existed and will always exist.

C. **Conclusion.** Thus ends one of the shortest and most controversial letters in the New Testament. It contains some of the harshest and most heated condemnations of false teachers in the Bible. It also encourages believers to stand strong in their faith and fight for it by living lifestyles of steadfast loyalty to the truth and merciful conduct toward those who are deceived by the lies of the world.

   1. But we also must understand that Jude's call to contend is not limited to battles for the faith solely against nonbelievers and false teachers in the church. It also includes contending for the faith within our own hearts and against the intrusion of false doctrine in our personal lives. We cannot allow compromise to enter into our families, careers, lifestyle, and other activities.

   2. Jude's letter reminds us that our beliefs directly impact how we act in all areas of our lives. Regardless of how societal norms and cultural standards change over time, God's truth never changes, and we are called to fight to ensure that His truths are faithfully taught and lived. They must always remain the basis for our own beliefs and conduct. It is that message which makes Jude still relevant to us today.

Questions for Personal Reflection or Group Discussion

1. *Jude 24:* What are two things listed by Jude that God is able to do for us? What comfort do these things give to you?

2. *Jude 25:* As you consider the attributes of God listed by Jude, how does his description of God impact your view of God?

3. *Jude 25:* Why do you think Jude chose to specify these particular attributes of God for the closing of his letter?

Notes

CHAPTER I
INTRODUCTION TO THE BOOK OF JUDE (JUDE 1-2)

1. Ray Summers, "Jude," The Broadman Bible Commentary, 12:232-239, gen. ed. Clifton J. Allen (Nashville, TN: Broadman Press, 1972), 232. The letter has had its critics, too. One commentator called it "the least valuable of the New Testament writings," while another said it has "little abiding spiritual significance." Ernest Findlay Scott, *The Literature of the New Testament* (New York, NY: Columbia University Press, 1948 reprint), 224 and T. Henshaw, *New Testament Literature in the Light of Modern Scholarship* (London, ENG: George Allen and Unwin, 1957 reprint), 391-392, both quoted in D. Edmond Hiebert, *Second Peter and Jude: An Expositional Commentary* (Greenville, SC: Unusual Publications, 1989), 205.

2. Jesus condemned the hypocritical attitude of the Pharisees in Mark 7:6-7: "Isaiah was right when he prophesied about you hypocrites; as it is written: 'These people honor me with their lips, but their hearts are far from me. They worship me in vain; their teachings are merely human rules'" (quoting Isaiah 29:13). To the complacent, Jesus said, "I know your deeds, that you are neither cold nor hot. I wish you were either one or the other! So, because you are lukewarm—neither hot nor cold—I am about to spit you out of my mouth" (Revelation 3:15-16).

3. Some scholars argue that the actual author was someone who used Jude's name as a pseudonym, but the evidence to support this argument is not as persuasive as those supporting the view that Jude himself is the author. See Richard J. Bauckham, *Jude, 2*

Peter, Word Biblical Commentary, vol. 50 (Waco, TX: Word Books, 1983), 21; Douglas J. Moo, *2 Peter, Jude,* The NIV Application Commentary (Grand Rapids, MI: Zondervan Publishing House, 1996), 27; Hiebert, 187.

4 See Moo, 222; J.N.D. Kelly, *A Commentary on the Epistles of Peter and of Jude* (Peabody, MA: Hendrickson Publishers, 1969), 242. Paul used the same title in his own writings. See, e.g., Romans 1:1; Philippians 1:1.

5 See Moo, 224-225.

6 The Roman Catholic Church teaches a Marian dogma that believes in Mary's "perpetual virginity." In other words, she was a virgin when Jesus was born and remained a virgin for the rest of her life. Therefore, the Catholic Church does not believe the brothers listed in Matthew 13:55 were children of Mary but instead were either cousins of Jesus (the Hieronymian view espoused by Jerome) or Joseph's children by a prior marriage (the Epiphanian view). The Greek word translated "brother," though, almost always means exactly that, so the best understanding of the passage is that Joseph and Mary had other children after the birth of Jesus. These brothers were, therefore, literally Jesus' half-brothers since Jesus had no earthly father. See Moo, 229; "The Four Marian Dogmas," *Catholic New Agency,* online at https://www.catholicnewsagency.com/resources/mary/general-information/the-four-marian-dogmas.

7 Eusebius, *Hist. Eccl.* 3:19.1-20.8 (available online at *Christian Classics Ethereal Library,* www.ccel.org/ccel/schaff/npnf201/Page_148.html). The truth of Hegesippus' account is suspect, but it may contain some elements of historical fact. Bauckham, 15.

8 Bauckham, 16. Syria is often mentioned as a possible location of the recipients, but Bauckham suggests it is unlikely since the churches in Syria were late in accepting Jude as part of the biblical canon.

9 Ibid., 26.

Notes

10 See Moo, 223.

11 Ibid., 224.

12 *Nelson's Complete Book of Bible Maps & Charts: Old and New Testaments* (Nashville, TN: Thomas Nelson Publishers, 1993), 478.

13 This is the view of Bauckham, Hiebert, and MacArthur. Bauckham, 143; Hiebert, 200; John MacArthur, Jr., *2 Peter & Jude,* The MacArthur New Testament Commentary (Chicago, IL: Moody Publishers, 2005), 145-146.

14 This is the view of Moo, Kelly, Summers, and Barclay. Moo, 18; Kelly 227; Summers, 234; William Barclay, *The Letters of John and Jude,* rev. ed., The Daily Bible Study Series (Louisville, KY: Westminster John Knox Press, 1976), 169.

15 This is the view of Cedar. Paul A. Cedar, *James; 1, 2 Peter; and Jude,* The Communicator's Commentary, vol. 11, gen. ed. Lloyd J. Ogilvie (Dallas, TX: Word Publishing, 1984), 245.

CHAPTER II
WARNINGS ABOUT FALSE TEACHERS (JUDE 3-16)

1 Cleon L. Rogers Jr. & Cleon L. Rogers III, *The New Linguistic and Exegetical Key to the Greek New Testament* (Grand Rapids, MI: Zondervan Publishing House, 1998), 605.

2 Moo, 229; see also Kelly, 247.

3 See Bauckham, 32.

4 Bauckham explains that people commonly mistake Jude's strong denunciations of the false teachers in verses 5-19 as setting an example of verbally accosting our opponents as the means of contending for the faith. But Bauckham says verses 5-19 are intended solely to make Jude's readers aware of the dangerous situation they faced. Only after highlighting the danger does Jude explain in verses 20-23 how they were to conduct themselves in the fight for the faith. Bauckham, 32.

63

5. See Bauckham, 32; Moo, 229; Kelly, 247; David Walls & Max Anders, *I & II Peter, I, II & III John, Jude,* Holman New Testament Commentary, vol. 11 (Nashville, TN: Broadman & Holman Publishers, 1999), 261.
6. See Bauckham, 34; Kelly 248.
7. Barclay, 178.
8. Ibid., 179.
9. See Hiebert, 222; Kelly, 249.
10. MacArthur, 158.
11. Ibid., 159. Scripture repeatedly warns us that the church's biggest threats are inside ones. For example, see Matthew 7:15, Acts 20:28-31, 2 Corinthians 11:13-15, Philippians 3:2, Colossians 2:18-19, 1 Timothy 1:6-7, 2 Peter 2:1, and 2 John 7. See also Aaron Armstrong, *Contend: Defending the Faith in a Fallen World* (Kindle version: Cruciform Press, Oct. 2012), 41.
12. MacArthur, 159.
13. Bauckham, 35-36; Moo, 230; Kelly 250. Other viewpoints are that their condemnation has already been recorded in the heavenly records and that their condemnation was prophesied earlier by the apostles. Bauckham, 35-36.
14. Bauckham, 38.
15. Kelly, 251.
16. Barclay, 180.
17. "New Book Describes the State of the Church in 2002," Barna (June 4, 2002), online at https://www.barna.com/research/new-book-describes-the-state-of-the-church-in-2002.
18. See Bauckham, 49; Moo, 248.
19. Bauckham, 51; Moo, 241; Fred D. Howard, *1, 2, & 3 John, Jude, Revelation,* Layman's Bible Book Commentary, vol. 24 (Nashville, TN: Broadman Press, 1982), 46; Julian Price Love, *The First,*

Notes

Second, and Third Letters of John; The Letter of Jude; The Revelation to John, The Layman's Bible Commentary, vol. 25 (Atlanta, GA: John Knox Press, 1960), 33. The question arises regarding whether Jude accepted and agreed with the story told in 1 Enoch and its description of the events in Genesis 6:1-4. It could be Jude was actually thinking of the stories in Isaiah 14:12-20 or Ezekiel 28:1-19, which are often interpreted as stories about fallen angels, or that he used the 1 Enoch story solely as a well-known illustration of his point without regard to its accuracy. Of course, there is also the possibility that Genesis 6:1-4 actually does involve fallen angels marrying human women. Moo, 111-112.

20 1 Enoch 6-19, available at Wesley Center Online (1995), http://wesley.nnu.edu/sermons-essays-books/noncanonical-literature/noncanonical-literature-ot-pseudepigrapha/book-of-enoch. The judgment of God for the angels' conduct was described in 1 Enoch 10:11-16: "And the Lord said unto Michael: 'Go, bind Semjaza and his associates who have united themselves with women so as to have defiled themselves with them in all their uncleanness. And when their sons have slain one another, and they have seen the destruction of their beloved ones, bind them fast for seventy generations in the valleys of the earth, till the day of their judgement and of their consummation, till the judgement that is for ever and ever is consummated. In those days they shall be led off to the abyss of fire: and to the torment and the prison in which they shall be confined forever. And whosoever shall be condemned and destroyed will from thenceforth be bound together with them to the end of all generations. And destroy all the spirits of the reprobate and the children of the Watchers, because they have wronged mankind. Destroy all wrong from the face of the earth and let every evil work come to an end: and let the plant of righteousness and truth appear: and it shall prove a blessing; the works of righteousness and truth shall be planted in truth and joy for evermore.'"

Bible Study Notes on Jude

21 The claim that homosexuality is not a sin is made despite the clear prohibitions of it and treatment of it as a perversion of God's laws in Genesis 19; Leviticus 18:22, 20:13; Romans 1:26-27; 1 Corinthians 6:9-10; 1 Timothy 1:9-10; and Jude 7.

22 Moo, 254.

23 Bauckham, 55; Kelly, 261. There are very strong condemnations and warnings in Scripture for those who teach falsehood on the basis of false prophetic dreams. See, e.g., Deuteronomy 13:1-5 and Colossians 2:18.

24 See Hiebert, 243.

25 There are only fragments of *The Assumption of Moses* (written probably around the first century A.D.) preserved today, none of which contain the story alluded to by Jude. However, other sources suggest the story was once part of the ending of the work and preserved the substance of the story in their retelling of it. Bauckham, 67. The lost ending is based upon the death and burial of Moses, which the Bible describes in Deuteronomy 34:5-6, where it says that "no one knows where his grave is." According to various accounts describing the lost ending, after Moses died, Michael was given the responsibility of burying his body. Satan, though, claimed Moses's body belonged to him. Michael refused to hand Moses's body over, Satan threatened to accuse Moses of being a murderer because he killed the Egyptian in Exodus 2:12. Michael did not rebuke Satan, however, but instead rebuked him on the basis of the Lord's authority, repeating the terminology used in Zech. 3:2. For a more detailed description of the story, see D.C. Arichea & H.A. Hatton, *A Handbook on the Letter from Jude and the Second Letter from Peter*, UBS NT Handbook Series (New York, NY: United Bible Societies), 1993, s.v. Jude 9; see full discussion about *The Assumption of Moses* in Bauckham, 65-76.

26 Bauckham, 79.

Notes

27 Josephus, *Antiquities of the Jews*, I.2:58, 61. Josephus wrote regarding Cain, "He did not accept of his punishment, in order to amendment, but to increase his wickedness; for he only aimed to procure everything that was for his own bodily pleasure, though it obliged him to be injurious to his neighbors. He augmented his household substance with much wealth, by rapine and violence; he excited his acquaintance to procure pleasures and spoils by robbery, and became a great leader of men into wicked courses." Ibid., I.2:60-61.

28 Bauckham, 81; Moo, 257; Kelly, 267. See 2 Peter 2:15.

29 Bauckham, 83; see also Barclay, 190.

30 Kelly, 269. Paul spoke of these meals in his complaint to the church at Corinth in 1 Corinthians 11:18-22.

31 Rogers & Rogers, 607;

32 Bauckham, 85-86; Moo, 258; Barclay, 193.

33 Bauckham, 87.

34 Moo, 260; Hiebert, 261. See Revelation 20:6.

35 See 1 Enoch 18:13-16: "I saw there seven stars like great burning mountains, and to me, when I inquired regarding them, the angel said: 'This place is the end of heaven and earth: this has become a prison for the stars and the host of heaven. And the stars which roll over the fire are they which have transgressed the commandment of the Lord in the beginning of their rising, because they did not come forth at their appointed times. And He was wroth with them, and bound them till the time when their guilt should be consummated (even) for ten thousand years.'" See also 1 Enoch 80:5-8: "[And in those days the sun shall be seen and he shall journey in the evening on the extremity of the great chariot in the west] And shall shine more brightly than accords with the order of light. And many chiefs of the stars shall transgress the order (prescribed). And these shall alter their orbits and tasks, And not appear at the seasons prescribed to

them. And the whole order of the stars shall be concealed from the sinners, And the thoughts of those on the earth shall err concerning them, [And they shall be altered from all their ways], Yea, they shall err and take them to be gods. And evil shall be multiplied upon them, And punishment shall come upon them So as to destroy all."

36 MacArthur, 181-182; Walls & Anders, 264; Kelly, 274. See also Bauckham, 90; Moo, 261.

37 See also 1 Enoch 27:2-3: "Then Uriel, one of the holy angels who was with me, answered and said: 'This accursed valley is for those who are accursed for ever: Here shall all the accursed be gathered together who utter with their lips against the Lord unseemly words and of His glory speak hard things. Here shall they be gathered together, and here shall be their place of judgement.'"

38 Jude's reliance upon and quotation of a nonbiblical, pseudepigraphal writing has elicited a lot of debate among scholars regarding whether the canon is truly closed, whether 1 Enoch is an inspired writing that should be in the canon, or whether Jude is inappropriately included in the canon due to his quotation of 1 Enoch. Clearly, 1 Enoch was a well-known writing in Jude's day that was popular among his readers, thus his quotation from it would have been impactful on his readers. There is no reason, however, to assume Jude thought it was canonical or actually written by Enoch. Like Paul (see e.g., Acts 17:28), Jude merely quoted from another source to make his point. As Hiebert suggests, the important issue is the accuracy of Jude's information as opposed to the source of it. Hiebert, 150. (For a discussion of the canonicity issue, see Moo, 271-274, 277-278.)

39 Lucian of Samosata, a first century Greek satirical writer and lecturer, described such grumbling in his work *The Cynic:* "You blessed ones are displeased with everything that happens and grumble without ceasing; what is is intolerable, what is not you pine for, in winter for summer, in summer for winter, in heat for

cold, in cold for heat, as fastidious and peevish as so many invalids; only their reason is to be found in their illness, and yours in your characters." Translation by H.W. Fowler and F.G. Fowler (1905), available online at http://www.sacred-texts.com/cla/luc/wl4/wl431.htm. A more contemporary translation might go like this: "You're satisfied by nothing that befalls you; you complain at everything. You don't want what you have got, you long for what you haven't got. In winter you wish it were summer, and in summer that it were winter. You are like the sick folk, hard to please, [always cursing your luck]." Michael Green, *2 Peter and Jude,* rev. ed., Tyndale New Testament Commentaries (Grand Rapids, MI: Wm. B. Eerdmans Publishing Co., 1987), 193.

40 Rogers & Rogers, 608.

41 Bauckham, 99-100.

CHAPTER III
STRATEGIES FOR CONTENDING FOR THE FAITH
(JUDE 17-23)

1 Scholars engage in lengthy discussions over who these "apostles" were, using the phrase to try to identify the date of Jude's writing. Some believe Jude referred to the actual Twelve (Hiebert, 274), while others believe Jude referenced the apostles who founded the churches to which Jude was writing (Bauckham, 104; Moo, 281).

2 Bauckham, 102. For instance, see Matthew 7:15; 2 Timothy 4:3-4; 2 Peter 2:1; 1 John 4:1.

3 Bauckham, 104.

4 Ibid.; Hiebert, 226; MacArthur, 199.

5 Moo, 280-281.

6 The six reasons identified in the following paragraphs a-f are summarized from MacArthur, 195-197.

7 Jude used two common triads in this passage: (1) faith, hope (i.e., mercy), and love and (2) Father, Son, and Holy Spirit. Moo, 284.

8 A. Duane Litfin, "A Biblical Strategy for Confronting the Cults," *Bibliotheca Sacra*, vol. 135 (July-Sept. 1978):232-240, p. 235.

9 Other translations say "*in* your most holy faith" (NIV, ESV, CSB), but the building imagery that Jude used clearly suggests that our faith (i.e., the essential doctrines of the Christian faith, as opposed to our beliefs and convictions) is to be the foundation upon which we build our lives. See Moo, 284.

10 Bauckham, 112; Moo, 284. See, e.g., 1 Thessalonians 5:11.

11 Moo, 284; Bauckham, 112.

12 Some teach "praying in the Spirit" refers to charismatic prayer that includes the practice of glossolalia or speaking in tongues. See, e.g., Bauckham, 113. But it is doubtful Jude had such a specific type of prayer in mind. It seems more likely Jude was speaking of prayer that is submitted to the will of the Holy Spirit and guided by Him. See Moo, 285.

13 T.W. Hunt, *The Doctrine of Prayer* (Nashville, TN: Convention Press, 1986), 46-47.

14 Bauckham, 114; Moo, 285.

15 Verses 22-23 are some of the most confusing passages in the New Testament. Some manuscripts and versions translate the passage with two clauses, while others have three clauses. Bauckham follows a two-clause translation of the text: "²²Snatch some from the fire, ²³but on those who dispute have mercy with fear, hating even the clothing that has been soiled by the flesh." Bauckham, 108; see also Kelly, 288. Most commentators, though, follow the three-clause translation that is used in NIV, ESV, NASB, and CSB. See, e.g., Moo, 286-287; Hiebert, 288; MacArthur, 202; Howard, 49; Barclay, 204.

16 Armstrong, 89.

17 Moo, 287-288.

18 See Hiebert, 289; MacArthur, 202.

19 Bauckham, 114; Moo, 288.

20 The Greek word Jude used that is translated "stained" means "filthy" and refers to human excrement. The Greek word for "clothing" refers to the garment that is worn next to the body. Thus, I interpret it as "dirty underwear." See also Moo, 289.

21 These are listed and summarized by Kevin DeYoung, "Jesus, Friend of Sinners: But How?" *The Gospel Coalition,* online at https://www.thegospelcoalition.org/blogs/kevin-deyoung/jesus-friend-of-sinners-but-how (Mar. 4, 2014).

22 Ibid.

23 Ryan Denison, "South Carolina city removes monument to fallen officers: How vocal should Christians be?" *Denison Forum,* online at https:/www.denisonforum.org/columns/daily-article/south-carolina-city-removes-monument-to-fallen-officers-how-vocal-should-christians-be (July 26, 2019). The remainder of this section 3.d. is summarized from Denison's blog post.

24 Ibid.

CHAPTER IV
DOXOLOGY (JUDE 24-25)

1 The word "doxology" is never used in the New Testament, but it was a common literary form in New Testament times. A doxology was commonly used to ascribe glory to God (the Greek word *doxa* means "glory"), especially at the end of a prayer, sermon, or letter. It is distinguished from a benediction, which usually started "blessed be God ...." Doxologies typically followed a four-element pattern: (1) identification of the one being praised (i.e., God); (2) words of praise that usually included a reference to glory; (3) a reference to time (such as "forever"); and (4) a concluding "Amen." Moo, 302.

2   Bauckham, 122; Moo, 300.

3   Barclay, 206.

4   Wayne Grudem, *Bible Doctrine: Essential Teachings of the Christian Faith* (Grand Rapids, MI: Zondervan, 1999), 304.

5   The recognition of God's uniqueness is part of the traditional Jewish confession in the Shemá: "Hear O Israel: the Lord our God, the Lord is one" (Deuteronomy 6:4).

6   Bauckham, 123.

7   The word "be" is not in the original text, but translators have added it. The supplied word could be "are," clearly making the list that follows a list of characteristics for God. But, as a doxology, "be" is probably more appropriate since it serves to recognize and praise Him for these characteristics. Moo, 301; Hiebert, 298.

8   Kelly, 293; Hiebert, 299.

9   Kelly, 293; Hiebert, 299.

10 There is some debate over whether the phrase "through Jesus Christ our Lord" modifies "Savior" or the list of attributes. If the former is what Jude intended, then Jude referred to Jesus as the mediator between God and mankind for salvation. If the latter was his meaning, then Jude referred to Jesus as the means through whom mankind acknowledges God's glory, majesty, power, and authority. Of course, both are true, so the debate is somewhat unnecessary, but within the context of a doxology, the latter is probably Jude's intended meaning. Bauckham, 123-124. See also Moo, 301; Kelly 292.

Sources Cited

Arichea, D.C. & H.A. Hatton. *A Handbook on the Letter from Jude and the Second Letter from Peter.* UBS NT Handbook Series. New York, NY: United Bible Societies. 1993.

Armstrong, Aaron. *Contend: Defending the Faith in a Fallen World.* Kindle version: Cruciform Press. Oct. 2012.

Barclay, William. *The Letters of John and Jude,* rev. ed. The Daily Bible Study Series. Louisville, KY: Westminster John Knox Press. 1976.

Bauckham, Richard J. *Jude, 2 Peter,* Word Biblical Commentary. Vol. 50. Waco, TX: Word Books. 1983.

Cedar, Paul A. *James; 1, 2 Peter; and Jude.* The Communicator's Commentary. Vol. 11. Lloyd J. Ogilvie, gen. ed. Dallas, TX: Word Publishing. 1984.

Denison, Ryan. "South Carolina city removes monument to fallen officers: How vocal should Christians be?" *Denison Forum.* July 26, 2019. Online at https:/www.denisonforum.org/columns/daily-article/south-carolina-city-removes-monument-to-fallen-officers-how-vocal-should-christians-be.

DeYoung, Kevin. "Jesus, Friend of Sinners: But How?" *The Gospel Coalition.* Mar. 4, 2019. Online at https://www.thegospelcoalition.org/blogs/kevindeyoung/jesus-friend-of-sinners-but-how.

Eusebius. *Hist. Eccl.* Available online at *Christian Classics Ethereal Library,* www.ccel.org/ccel/schaff/npnf201/Page_148.html.

"The Four Marian Dogmas." *Catholic New Agency.* Accessed July 2, 2019. Online at https://www.catholicnewsagency.com/resources/mary/general-information/the-four-marian-dogmas.

Lucian of Samosata. *The Cynic.* Translation by H.W. Fowler & F.G. Fowler (1905). Available online at http://www.sacred-texts.com/cla/luc/wl4/wl431.htm.

Green, Michael. *2 Peter and Jude,* rev. ed. Tyndale New Testament Commentaries. Grand Rapids, MI: Wm. B. Eerdmans Publishing Co. 1987.

Grudem, Wayne. *Bible Doctrine: Essential Teachings of the Christian Faith.* Grand Rapids, MI: Zondervan. 1999.

Henshaw, T. *New Testament Literature in the Light of Modern Scholarship.* London, ENG: George Allen and Unwin. 1957 reprint.

Hiebert, D. Edmond. *Second Peter and Jude: An Expositional Commentary.* Greenville, SC: Unusual Publications. 1989.

Howard, Fred D. *1, 2, & 3 John, Jude, Revelation.* Layman's Bible Book Commentary. Vol. 24. Nashville, TN: Broadman Press. 1982.

Hunt, T.W. *The Doctrine of Prayer.* Nashville, TN: Convention Press. 1986.

Josephus, *Antiquities of the Jews.*

Kelly, J.N.D. *A Commentary on the Epistles of Peter and of Jude.* Peabody, MA: Hendrickson Publishers. 1969.

Sources Cited

Litfin, A. Duane. "A Biblical Strategy for Confronting the Cults." *Bibliotheca Sacra.* Vol. 135. July-Sept. 1978:232-240.

Love, Julian Price. *The First, Second, and Third Letters of John; The Letter of Jude; The Revelation to John.* The Layman's Bible Commentary. Vol. 25. Atlanta, GA: John Knox Press. 1960.

MacArthur, Jr., John. *2 Peter & Jude.* The MacArthur New Testament Commentary. Chicago, IL: Moody Publishers. 2005.

Moo, Douglas J. *2 Peter, Jude.* The NIV Application Commentary. Grand Rapids, MI: Zondervan Publishing House. 1996.

Nelson's Complete Book of Bible Maps & Charts: Old and New Testaments. Nashville, TN: Thomas Nelson Publishers. 1993.

"New Book Describes the State of the Church in 2002." *Barna.com.* June 4, 2002. Online at https://www.barna.com/research/new-book-describes-the-state-of-the-church-in-2002.

Rogers Jr., Cleon L. & Cleon L. Rogers III. *The New Linguistic and Exegetical Key to the Greek New Testament.* Grand Rapids, MI: Zondervan Publishing House. 1998.

Scott, Ernest Findlay. *The Literature of the New Testament.* New York, NY: Columbia University Press. 1948.

Summers, Ray. "Jude." The Broadman Bible Commentary. Vol. 12. Clifton J. Allen, gen. ed. Nashville, TN: Broadman Press. 1972.

Walls, David & Max Anders. *I & II Peter, I, II & III John, Jude.* Holman New Testament Commentary. Vol. 11. Nashville, TN: Broadman & Holman Publishers. 1999.

Also by the Author

Lessons from Solomon: Finding True Success in Life provides an engaging and thought-provoking look at the life of King Solomon in the Bible and draws specific lessons from his vast life experiences—both the successes and the failures—that we can apply in our own personal quests to find true success in life.

The book is available in hardcover, softcover, and eBook formats wherever books are sold online. You can also find the book on the author's website at www.glenblanscet.com.

"Based on the life of Solomon, Blanscet has distilled from Solomon's story the life lessons that lead us to genuine success from the wisest man who ever lived. I highly recommend this book!"

Dr. David Allen
Dean of the School of Preaching
Southwestern Baptist Theological Seminary

www.ingramcontent.com/pod-product-compliance
Lightning Source LLC
Chambersburg PA
CBHW071024080526
44587CB00015B/2485